ALL ABOUT
SAGUAROS

Text by Carle Hodge

Photography by *Arizona Highways* Contributors

Edited by Wesley Holden and Robert J. Farrell

Design and Production by W. Randall Irvine

Cover Design by Russ Wall

ARIZONA
HIGHWAYS

(ABOVE) *View of Tucson from Tumamoc Hill, where the Carnegie Institution established its Desert Laboratory in 1902. The facility served as headquarters for much of the early study of saguaros.* JACK DYKINGA

Prepared by the Book Division of *Arizona Highways* magazine,
a monthly publication of the Arizona Department of Transportation.
Nina M. La France-Publisher / Bob Albano-Managing Editor / Robert J. Farrell-Associate Editor / Cindy Mackey-Production Manager
Third printing 1996. Revisions by Leo Banks.

Library of Congress Catalog Number 91 070844
ISBN 0-916179-60-5

TABLE OF CONTENTS

Nothing so symbolizes the Southwestern lowlands as a single plant, the saguaro. This giant cactus has become a desert icon beloved by cartoonists, photographers, and movie-makers and familiar even to foreigners who never will see one.

To millions, Arizona is spelled s-a-g-u-a-r-o. Pronounce it suh-WAR-oh, a Spanish corruption of a term given it by ancient Indians who tapped its fruit for food and drink. The cactus lives upwards of a century and a half — perhaps as long as 200 years — and can weigh two tons and more. The most aged of those now silhouetted against the horizon made their way into this inhospitable environment when it was still a remote part of the realm of King Charles IV of Spain, yet to be deposed from the throne by Napoleon. Some saguaros living today possibly arose when Arizona was part of Mexico, territory the United States would not acquire until 1853.

The largest cactus in the United States (the cardon of Mexico is taller and several South American species more massive) can thrust up to 40 feet and more. Leafless and spiny, it is encased in a thick green waxy skin that retards evaporation and is vertically pleated to permit expansion when water is available. Despite the fact the plants put out branches, from a distance the skyscraping cactuses give an impression of great Greek columns — or armies of green Goliaths marching away into infinity.

Sheer size accounts partly for the plant's prominence, where on the desert trees seldom exceed scruffy bushes in height. But another explanation exists for its almost mythic place in the Arizona psyche. To many desert dwellers, saguaros possess a human quality, an imagery that promotes an affection bestowed on few plants. Artists like to portray them with sombreros and sunglasses. Residents take fierce pride in specimens in their yards and react angrily when one is harmed.

(LEFT) *Sunset highlights a craggy peak peering over a dense forest of saguaros near Tucson.* WILLARD CLAY

(ABOVE) *A monarch stands sentinel as the distant lights of Phoenix twinkle on the evening horizon.* RICK ODELL

Mid-1990 saw the "Great Saguaro Rush" northwest of Phoenix to Lake Pleasant, which the federal Bureau of Reclamation was enlarging to hold water for the Central Arizona Project. When the agency offered saguaros to persons willing to remove them from the land to be flooded, 4,000 families applied within a few weeks.

This passion pervades the language as well. People speak more of saguaro "arms" than branches. Seedlings, so minuscule they are difficult at best to see, become "babies," and even scientists who spend careers studying saguaros refer to the shrubs and trees beneath which the seeds germinate as "nurse plants." Schools, streets, and businesses are named for the desert monarch. The Phoenix telephone directory lists the word more than 60 times.

For all the attention given it, however, the saguaro remains a tower of paradox. The very quintessence of desert flora, it nonetheless can take hold only where there is shade and moisture; moreover, some of the semi-desert habitats where it now thrives may become too dry for it. And as evocative of the entire American West as it is to many people, it actually inhabits a limited range.

Botanist Forrest Shreve was first to delineate this region. Shreve worked as a staff member at the old Desert Laboratory, an outpost the Carnegie Institution of Washington maintained in Tucson for several decades in the early 1900's. He determined that, except for three isolated, rather sparse sites on California's side of the Colorado River, the species may be seen in this country only in Arizona. Its range spreads northwestward as far as the Hualapai Mountains near Kingman and from the Colorado east to the Galiuro Mountains northeast of Tucson. It is missing in the driest parts of our state and at loftier elevations where frost may prevail 24 hours at a time. In Mexico, which has the majority of saguaros, they dot the arid terrain as far south as the Rio Mayo in the state of Sonora.

But Shreve also presented a riddle which has yet to be fully resolved. He observed very few small saguaros around the laboratory, and from that he surmised the big cactuses were failing to repopulate. We now know the pioneering botanist was only partly correct, that there is reproduction in some areas but little or none in others. The reasons remain somewhat elusive.

Although no one before had solved or even discovered so many saguaro mysteries, Shreve and

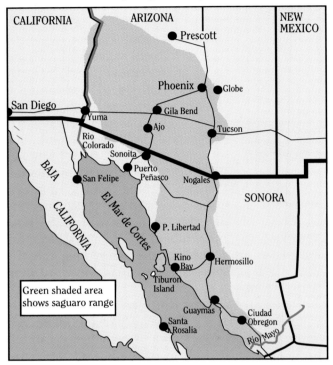

CALIFORNIA   ARIZONA   NEW MEXICO

● Prescott

Phoenix ● Globe

San Diego

Yuma ● Gila Bend
Rio Colorado ● Ajo   ● Tucson
Sonoita
Puerto Peñasco   Nogales
San Felipe

BAJA CALIFORNIA

El Mar de Cortes

SONORA

● P. Libertad

Kino Bay   ● Hermosillo
Tiburon Island

Guaymas   ● Ciudad Obregon
Santa Rosalia
Rio Mayo

Green shaded area shows saguaro range

his colleagues at the laboratory were not the first to make observations about this plant. In 1540, Coronado's conquistadors, the first Europeans to penetrate the desert Southwest, wrote about a giant cactus they called "pitahaya."

More than 200 years ensued, though, before the plant first was described in a scientific journal. In 1848, George Engelmann at the Missouri Botanical Gardens in St. Louis christened it *Cereus giganteus*. Then more than a half-century later, two famous Eastern botanists, Nathaniel Lord Britton and Joseph Nelson Rose, spent four years at the New York Botanical Garden, in the Bronx, overhauling the classification of cactuses. They cataloged 123 genera and renamed the saguaro *Carnegiea gigantea*, presumably in tribute to the generous funding steel magnate Andrew Carnegie devoted to desert research.

That latter appelation prevails, particularly since scientists proved in the 1970's that saguaros do not belong in the genus *cereus*. The giant is, however, a distant generic cousin of two smaller column-growing cactuses found along the Mexican

border, the senita and the organ pipe.

But dissent over its name pales beside a philosophical controversy that has rumbled over three decades between ecologists and plant pathologists at the University of Arizona, in Tucson. Their rift centers on the dramatic die-off of saguaros in certain areas and whether to blame brutal cold or bacterial disease. Each side claims enough clues to satisfy itself, if not the unconverted.

That the debate arose at all illuminates the intensity of saguaro investigations, many of them at the UofA during the past 30 years. (After the research of Shreve and his associates, scientists fairly ignored the species until the 1940s.) But much has been learned, not the least of which is that it never is too late to be surprised by what one learns.

Almost anyone even casually acquainted with saguaros knows they expand or contract as they gain or lose moisture. During droughts, their ribs show like those of a prospector adrift on the dunes. During the summer rainy season, the plants puff up like balloons, the pleats in their sides widening like bellows. Just how much watery girth a giant could add, though, remained uncertain.

James Rodney Hastings, a geoclimatologist on the Tucson campus homed in on Shreve's old workplace, the Desert Laboratory on Tumamoc Hill, on Tucson's western edge. Using sensitive instruments on living specimens, he came up with an awesome number. One saguaro he measured fattened from 31 inches in circumference to 47 inches during a single summer. Such adaptability explains how the species can survive many months without water, continuing to flower and fruit in the driest of periods, and often even after a giant has toppled.

(RIGHT) *The primary purpose of saguaro spines is to discourage predators from damaging the plant. In addition, closely grouped spines provide sparse shade for the plant's growing tip. In ways not fully fathomed, spines may help regulate internal temperatures. Examination of mature plants (A) shows that spines grow from hairy lateral buds (areoles) on the edges of the ribs. Spines change color as they get older. Flexible yellow spines (B) appear near growing tips. Descending the saguaro, spines become brown, then black and increasingly brittle. (C) This photo compares young and old. On old saguaros, the lower trunk may become bark-like. Since spines are no longer needed to protect the plant, they fall or are easily bumped off. Bark is the result of age and, since more appears on the south face, "sunburn."*

A   WILLARD CLAY

B   WESLEY HOLDEN

C   WESLEY HOLDEN

Saguaro roots sprawl outward over a distance approximately equal to the plant's height. Still, there's a price for the ability to hoard water for thirsty times. Lace-like roots that proliferate near the surface permit the plant to blot up the blessing of even scant rain. On slopes, the long radial roots wind among rocks and brace the saguaro against ordinary winds. But a small, shallow root network provides a poor anchor in a windstorm, and not infrequently a giant is blown down. And when the plant is weighty with water, the menace increases.

Another puzzle had been how fast saguaros grow. If a visitor asks, he may get as many answers as the number of natives he queries. Favorite local legends cite growth ranging from an inch a year to an inch a month. The correct answer is not so simple, of course, nor so predictable.

Growth varies from location to location and from year to year, depending on temperature, moisture, soil conditions, elevation, and other factors, not the least being the age of a particular plant. The rate differs at different stages in the saguaro life span. At any time, progress is ponderously slow. At Saguaro National Monument east of Tucson, a seedling needs more than five years to poke up an inch out of the ground. At Organ Pipe Cactus National Monument, a lower and drier location, it takes almost twice that long. As a rough rule of thumb, an adult saguaro east of Tucson should stand a bit above 12 feet at age 50, 22 feet at 75, and a little more than 30 at 100 years.

Nearly all the experts agree that where there is saguaro repopulation, it most often takes place not on the flatlands, but on the lower rocky slopes of the mountains — *bajadas* — where the soil retains moisture more efficiently. Slowly, then, scientists are deciphering the saguaro's secrets.

They have shown its nocturnal flower to be an overnight sensation, a creamy-white spectacle that seldom lasts until a second dusk. Through elaborate experiments they learned that birds and bees pollinate it by day, and bats by night. Further, they

found that almost no seeds remain uneaten by predators, that germination can occur only during the monsoon storms of summer, and that the chances a seedling will survive six weeks are odds no Las Vegas gambler would consider.

Although the saguaro's prospects for a full lifetime grow more promising with age, it's still a desert out there. Disease, winter cold, wildfires, and lightning threaten these giants. But perhaps its greatest threat comes from humans. Woodcutters chop — and cattle chew — the trees small saguaros need for shelter. Vandals attack saguaros. Thieves steal them for sale on the black market. Developers pave prime habitat. Even for a monarch, life can be treacherous.

For all of these reasons researchers remain fascinated, not only with understanding the saguaro, but also with what this knowledge might reveal about the interrelationships of all life in so pitiless an environment.

(INSET) *Author Carle Hodge examines a saguaro boot. A veteran* Arizona Highways *contributor, the late Hodge covered science for* The Arizona Daily Star, The Arizona Republic, *and other publications.*
DAVID ELMS, JR.

(TOP) *A lone Goliath towers above a golden grove of flowering paloverde trees south of the Galiuro Mountains, the plant's easternmost habitat. Paloverdes are but one variety of plants that serve as "nurse," shading young saguaros.* CHRISTINE KEITH

On the evolutionary calendar, cactuses generally, and saguaros certainly, are newcomers. Exactly how long the cactus family has been around probably will never be known. The oldest North American cactus fossil dated so far, a prickly-pear fragment unearthed in western Arizona, is at least 40,000 years old. Although that is as far back as radiocarbon dating can reach, it is still, geologically speaking, barely yesterday.

Circumstantial evidence, however, allows cactologists to infer that these distinctly New World natives originated near the equatorial latitudes around 67 million years ago, a time roughly 2 million years after the dinosaurs disappeared and when most flowering plants already were established.

Cactuses probably descended from short, inconspicuous tropical trees that forfeited their leaves and became dormant during droughts. During the 40 or so million years that followed in that early Tertiary time, primitive cactuses began acquiring the characteristics that would permit them to persevere.

While fault-blocking was lifting the basin-and-range mountain chains across the desert Southwest between 10 and 30 million years ago, major cactus genera, still restricted close to the equator, became recognizable. That happened amid an overall cooler, drier period which hastened plant evolution.

Between 3 million and 10 million years before the present, the climate dried still more and divided into seasons. Cactuses expanded widely both north and south of the tropics, and the ancestral saguaro and its columnar cousins manifested themselves.

Recognizably modern species came into being 1 million to 3 million years ago in both North and South America. *Carnegiea gigantea*, the saguaro, arrived in the Sonoran Desert at the same time the similar cardon, *Trichocereus terschecki*, arrived in the Monte Desert of northwestern Argentina, which itself is a Sonoran Desert look-alike.*

Present-day cactus distribution was pretty much fixed after the end of the last Ice Age, around 11,000 years ago, when the final glaciers retreated northward. The climate warmed, and the Bermuda High strengthened. This great high-pressure system, perched over the Atlantic Ocean most of the year, spins westward each spring and summer brewing monsoon moisture. Without this, there would be no saguaros in the Southwest.

So over those many millions of years, cactuses (from the Greek word for thistles) evolved into an awesome variety of sizes and shapes, from gargantuan to almost infinitesimal. By definition, all cactuses share characteristics. First, they must have areoles, the small oval pits from which grow spines (and often miniscule hairs, or glochids), flowers, and eventually fruit. The areole distinguishes cactuses from other plants. Second, cactuses are perennial, requiring more than one season to mature and flower. Third, all have flowers which are usually wheel-shaped or funnel-shaped. Fourth, the fruit that develops from the flower has one compartment, with seeds distributed through the pulp at random. Fifth, all cactus seeds, following germination, produce two embryo leaves. Finally, a cactus can reproduce from cuttings as well as from seeds.

There may be as many as 1,200 cactus species. Although primarily intolerant of cold, cactuses grow as far north as British Columbia and in all but five of the United States. Clumps of prickly pears even cling to the dunes near the eastern end of New York's Long Island.

(LEFT) *The aroma of damp creosote bushes perfumes the air as a summer storm drenches the usually parched desert soil near Cave Creek. Saguaros, through their extensive shallow root system, can absorb enough water to last a year or more from one such rain.* JERRY JACKA

(ABOVE) *Lightning wreaths some desert old-timers, promising the advent of crucial moisture.* WILLARD CLAY

*This is an excellent example of "ecological equivalents," plants and animals that occupy different geographical areas but have been shaped by similar environments. Other cases: paloverde, desert hackberry, and creosote bushes cover both the Sonoran and the Monte deserts. American sidewinder snakes propel themselves the same way as the sand vipers and sand adders of Africa.

Arizona claims more than 70 kinds, second in number only to Texas. Of all these, though, only two in the United States are even remotely related to the saguaro: the organ pipe cactus and the senita cactus which grow mainly in or near Organ Pipe Cactus National Monument. Like saguaros, they ascend in tree-like columns. Organ pipe cactuses were named for an obvious reason. They erect a bundle of stems — usually 15 to 20 and up to 30 feet high — that rise from a base several feet thick.

Senitas, which look like small organ pipe cactuses, are known as the "whisker cactus," from the gray, beard-like knot of scruffy spines along the edges of the upper ribs of older branches. Senitas grow in clumps, may have 100 or more branches, and reach 21 feet in height. The two also differ in that the senita is more serrated, and the ridges on the trunk are deeper than the rounder organ pipe.

(RIGHT) *Saguaros thrive at Organ Pipe Cactus National Monument next to one of the Park's namesake plants.* WILLARD CLAY

(BELOW) *Related species of cactuses, the cardon, saguaro, and senita, from left to right, rise together near the Mexican border.* DAVID BURCKHALTER

Nature allots a surprisingly short time for pollination of Arizona's state flower. Each saguaro blossom slowly unfolds a few hours after sunset in May or early June. By the following afternoon or, infrequently, the afternoon of the second day, the creamy-white chalice closes forever.

That the pollen grains are too heavy to be windborne was established decades ago. Later, scientists determined that the blooms must be fertilized by microspores from another saguaro or from another arm of the same saguaro. This they learned by carefully hand-pollinating the plant, using camel's-hair brushes to dab on the tiny particles.

Obviously there had to be natural agents for distributing the pollen. By caging domestic honey bees with flowering saguaros, it was found that bees, if they are abundant, cross-pollinate the cactus. The insects submerge themselves in the petals to collect sugary nectar, which saguaros produce in far greater abundance than most plants. When the bees dart away, they are coated with white dust-like pollen.

But the mystery wasn't really solved. Because honey bees were not imported into the Southwest until 1872, they could not have accounted for the present-day stands of aging cactuses. Other pollinators had to be identified. One candidate was the western white-winged dove, a migrant from Mexico whose northernmost territory in the spring matches that of the saguaro. It seemed likely, moreover, since the flowers endure so briefly, that some pollination occurred at night.

So, UofA plant pathologist Stanley Alcorn, National Park Service naturalist George Olin, and their co-workers tried another cage test. This time, in addition to blooming saguaros, the enclosure also contained flowering stalks of the shin-dagger agave,

(LEFT) A saguaro in full flower springs from volcanic boulders in the Superstition Mountains. To save water, saguaro sap is thick and gummy. DAVID MUENCH

(ABOVE) Arizona's state flower. GEORGE H.H. HUEY

or amole. Bees and white-wings were placed separately in the enclosure followed by another animal, the long-nose bat found at Colossal Cave near Tucson. The long-nose was included because saguaro pollen had been located in its stomach and feces.

Small and brownish, with short, round ears and a truncated tail, long-nose bats winter in Mexico, arriving in southern Arizona about the time the saguaros flower. Unlike most of their order, which eat insects, the long-noses feed upon nectar, a dietary mode to which they are peculiarly adapted by virtue of a bristly tongue that often extends a quarter the length of the body.

All three of these creatures — the bees, the birds, the bats — were released in turn into the pen. Like the bees and doves, the bats inadvertently dispersed pollen as they flitted from flower to flower on their nectar-gathering forays, the pollen often turning their small, furry heads white.

Before burrowing into the blossoms, the winged mammals hovered above for several seconds, in much the manner of hummingbirds. At other times, they clambered clumsily from one flower to another. Often they left the snowy pollen of the saguaro mixed with the yellow of the agave, suggesting the same bats visited both plants.

The bats, therefore, performed by night the same ecological role the birds and bees played by day. While this was no surprise, it turned out the bats were especially effective. For inexplicably, although the bees and birds were exposed to more flowers, more fruit set (fertilization of the flowers resulting in fruit) occurred in the flowers visited by the bats.

By no means did these investigations eliminate the possibility that in the field other pollinators take part in this magic of multiplication. Scientists would, indeed, be astonished if many others do not, including several kinds of wild bees.

Each adult saguaro engenders about half a dozen flowers a day for some 30 days. Usually half the flowers set, the scarlet fruit ripening about 37 days after the first blossoms appear. Because the

plant hoards an incredible quantity of water — the Desert Laboratory's Forrest Shreve called it "the cactus camel" — the reproduction process can, and often does, happen during the hottest and driest weeks of the year.

The first splash of white blooms among the crowns varies by weeks from year to year, as the stands await the arrival of vernal warmth. And at separate elevations and latitudes flowering takes place at different times, a function of temperature variations. Even as short a distance as the 30 miles between the two segments of Saguaro National Park reflects this. Spring, and blooming, arrive at the west unit a week or two earlier than at the original refuge to the east, which is some 500 feet higher.

In Mexico, 10 days may pass between the first flowering along the Gulf of California and that on the mountain slopes near Hermosillo, Sonora, 50 miles inland and more than 2,000 feet above sea level.

Consequently, fruit ripens later in some locales than in others. But by late July in most places the Sonoran Desert is awash with red. The stately saguaro, seemingly timeless from a human perspective, has embarked on another year.

(ABOVE) *Their faces dusted with saguaro pollen, lesser long-nosed bats feed on nectar. Death-by-pesticide of many bats may diminish pollination of the big cactuses. That might unravel the whole web of desert life in which the saguaro plays a key role.* MERLIN D. TUTTLE, Bat Conservation International

(ABOVE RIGHT) *Curve-billed thrashers, noisy natives of Southwestern lowlands, also eat from the flower.* JIM HONCOOP

(RIGHT) *Another pollinator, the white-winged dove, dines on the saguaro's fruit.* C. ALLAN MORGAN

(FOLLOWING PANEL, PAGES 18 AND 19) *Where giants prevail. Virtual groves of saguaros top the Tucson Mountains. These mountains harbor the most robust* Carnegiea *stands.* PETER KRESAN

ILLUSTRATIONS BY WENDY HODGESON

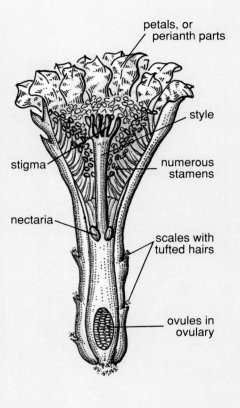

petals, or
perianth parts

style

stigma

numerous
stamens

nectaria

scales with
tufted hairs

ovules in
ovulary

dried perianth
parts (petals, etc)

seeds
embedded
in pulp

areole
(more felted in
younger growth)

one
central
spine

radial
spines

A MONUMENTAL FOREST

Homer Shantz had a dilemma. As president of the University of Arizona, he had too little money and more land than he could pay off. The Great Depression was descending, and his faculty worried about jobs and grumbled about pay.

No one deprecated his romance with the property. There, on the western face of the Rincon Mountains, 17 miles east of downtown Tucson, ruled a regal spread of saguaros, including one extravagant grove called the Cactus Forest.

Nor did many object that Shantz, a botanist of global renown long before he ran a university, had invested state funds on a down payment for the parcel of 5.5 sections — 3,520 acres — which clearly cried for defense. Cattle trampled it. Prospectors picked at it. And even then, in the ebbing 1920's, the noose of humanity threatened the area. (In 1929, Tucson still had a population of only 26,000; and Phoenix, 38,000). If a scientist was not to save this *rara avis*, who was?

Still, one must face financial reality. Shantz recruited the publisher of *The Tucson Citizen*, Frank Hitchcock, and together they enlisted help from Washington, D. C. After years of dealing, state land was added to federal land, and federal land bartered for private plots. Finally, President Hoover signed Saguaro National Monument into reality in March of 1933, three days before departing the White House. What was to become Saguaro National Monument East then belonged to the U.S Forest Service — for 13 days. The new chief executive, Franklin D. Roosevelt, then assigned it and 15 other monuments to the National Park Service. The monument was

Photographs taken decades apart of an area known as the "Cactus Forest" dramatically document population decline at Saguaro National Monument East.

(TOP LEFT) *The area in 1935.*
NATIONAL PARK SERVICE PHOTO

(BOTTOM, LEFT) *The same setting in 1965.*
NATIONAL PARK SERVICE PHOTO BY J.R. HASTINGS

(BELOW) *The scene in 1991.* DAVID ELMS, JR.

designated a national park October 14, 1994.

The refuge now reaches far beyond Shantz's dream. It stretches up to the nearly 9,000-foot summit of the Rincons and encompasses much more than cactuses. From a distance the Rincons resemble a dun-colored cardboard cutout stage set. Up close, they transform into a world apart, bristling with cactus species beyond belief and studded with low shrubs and trees.

In spring, if there has been sufficient winter rain, brittlebush paint a patina of gold, flowering paloverdes yellow the slopes, and ocotillos wave red-tipped wands. In summer, huge masses of darkening anvil-shaped clouds tower thousands of feet above the stony backdrop of the Rincons, thunderously promising the advent of life-giving storms. Gentle desert tortoises lumber off in search of prickly-pear fruit. Roadrunners, foxes, and coyotes dart though the mesquites. Hawks navigate updrafts. Javelinas and bobcats roam the range.

Shantz, a few years after the Park was set aside, wrote rapturously about this "wild, weird place" in *National Geographic* magazine. To him, "the prevailing color of the entire area was green, the mesquite an olive-green, the saguaro a light olive."

By then he had left Tucson to become the Forest Service wildlife boss. Although his article was a first-person account, he did not hint of his own role in the incomplete drama.

Schantz's legacy was laced with a touch of trepidation. Even before the original 99-square-mile Monument was established, researchers recognized the Cactus Forest was past its prime. The year 1939 revealed one likely reason. That February entered the annals as the coldest ever in Tucson, and within months scientists diagnosed rot among the giants. Could they attribute the decline to periodic freezes? To the rot alone?

DAVID ELMS, JR. INGE MARTIN

DAVID ELMS, JR.

DAVID ELMS, JR.

CHARLES BUSBY

WESLEY HOLDEN

Year-round running water is rare on the Sonoran Desert.

(LEFT) *Saguaros line the Verde River near Red Creek in the Tonto National Forest northeast of Phoenix.* DAVID ELMS, JR.

(ABOVE) *Saguaros cling to a cliff amid blooming paloverdes above Sabino Creek in the Santa Catalina Mountains northeast of Tucson.*
DAVID W. LAZAROFF

MONARCHS WITH CROWNS

Few plants exceed the saguaro cactus in strangeness. But some rare saguaros are even more bizarre because of the crowns they wear. These abnormal crested, or cristate, individuals can be readily identified by their gnarled, fan-shaped comb-like tops. Instead of branching as normal saguaros do, the crested plant's growing tip — the apex — goes awry. How often this occurs, no one can be certain. It probably affects something like one out of every 200,000 saguaros.

Researchers disagree as to the cause or causes. Some suggest genetic quirks, others lightning strikes. But the best bet is damage to the apex either mechanically or from freezing. Whatever the explanation, the cristates definitely are the oddest of this unusual family.

(LEFT) *One of the larger cristate giants known, this resident of Organ Pipe Cactus National Monument spreads its gnarled crown approximately 7 feet, 10 inches across.*

(ABOVE) *A side view of same specimen.*
Note the "seam" where front and back meet.
PHOTOGRAPHS BY DAVID ELMS, JR.

(RIGHT) *Twin combs distinguish this unique cactus.*
WESLEY HOLDEN

C. ALLAN MORGAN

WESLEY HOLDEN

▲ FRANK ZULLO

▼ TOM BEAN

DAVID ELMS, JR.

Saguaros with convoluted crowns appear in almost every imaginable form and throughout the entire growing region of the plant. The photos on these pages illustrate the overall appearance of the plant along with a close-up detail of the cristated portion.

In a study of the saguaro's unlikely debut and improbable early years, a National Park Service scientist once painstakingly separated almost 50,000 seeds from the ripe red fruits in which they were impasted. (One fruit may hold 2,200 or more glossy, reddish-black seeds, which are so small it would take at least 380 of them to outweigh an aspirin.)

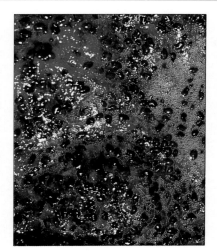

Biologist Warren F. (Scotty) Steenbergh first washed the seeds free from the pulp, then hand-counted them into lots of 1,000 and scattered each lot over a carefully marked-off test plot. The object was to see why so many simply vanish.

The answer came quickly in one test. Large red harvester ants swarmed from a nest some 70 feet away and, in a herculean feat of freight handling, began removing the specks. In little more than an hour not one of the 1,000 seeds remained in sight.

Although this frustration merely typified many that Steenbergh encountered, the incident illustrates the lengths to which cactologists have gone to resolve the riddles of Arizona's most famous plant — and the obstacles Nature puts in its path.

To ensure a permanent population, a parent plant over its entire lifetime need replicate itself only once, bequeathing a copy that manages to persist until, at about age 30, it can make its own seeds. As simple as this requisite sounds, the odds against its happening almost tax credibility.

(ABOVE LEFT) *Potential saguaro giants, left to right, two weeks, one week, and three weeks old. Year-old seedlings weigh less than an aspirin, and in the wild, stand a less than one in several million chance of germinating and surviving to adulthood. But in the controlled conditions of a saguaro greenhouse, better than 90 percent of the seeds become thriving cactuses.* JIM HONCOOP

(LOWER LEFT) *Potted plants ranging in age from five months to five years.* WESLEY HOLDEN

(ABOVE) *Seeds still embedded, watermelon-like, in fruit.* DAVID ELMS, JR.

An average adult saguaro produces 100 fruits a year. Steenbergh and Charles Lowe, a UofA ecologist, calculated that a healthy saguaro, during a century of fertility, bears 40 million seeds. Despite this awesome proliferation, perils lurk at every step.

Late-winter freezes, first of all, are harbingers of doom at the very genesis of the plant's life span. Cold can nip the new buds or ambush sprouting seedlings. Strangely, heat kills, too. Because the spring's first high temperatures trigger fruiting, earlier-than-normal warmth exposes seeds to predation for a longer time. Usually, though, fruit ripening and seedfall peak in late June or early July. In one of Nature's multitude of miracles, that moment precedes by days, or at most, a few weeks, the rush of summer rains required for germination.

Besides enabling the potential giants to germinate, the monsoons perform another role. Summer downpours fell fruit still attached to the plant and sweep the seeds downslope to microhabitats — the shade of rocks or trees or bushes — where the newborns can withstand the withering heat to come.

The dramatic disappearance of the tiny seeds starts even before the thunderstorms explode over the horizon and continues through and past the rainy season. Less than a single seed out of every 1,000 lasts long enough to sprout.

Animals devour most of them. But the creatures affect the plant's fate both negatively and positively. Almost every desert dweller, from the harvester ants Steenbergh studied to coyotes and pig-like javelinas (peccaries), feasts on the fruit and seed. How many seeds specific species consume, though, differs from one locale to another.

In the Cactus Forest portion of Saguaro National Park East, ants and the abundant round-tailed ground squirrels take the most. By contrast, those residents are fewer on the lower, drier western Monument, and more seeds survive there. About 95 percent of the coyote scat collected one July in the Tucson area was made up of saguaro seeds. So was 85 percent of the javelina droppings.

Birds also feast on the fruit and seed. Among these are Gambel's quail, cactus wrens, and gilded flickers, but mainly the same white-winged doves that helped pollinate the plants only weeks earlier. While some birds and animals, such as doves and kangaroo rats, digest the seeds, others do not. Seeds pass, still viable, through the digestive tracts of ground squirrels, wood rats, coyotes, and certain birds, and drop again to the ground, bestowing a second chance at germination and the beginnings of a tenuous life.

Stanley Alcorn, a University of Arizona plant pathologist, and National Park Service naturalist George Olin found that white-wings also spill some seeds to the surface as they regurgitate meals to their nesting young. This deposits the seed beneath sheltering branches. Another example of symbiosis: Avian and mammal droppings spread seed upslope and on the flatlands where they would not have been swept by the summer's first downpours.

Still, not all seeds reach a hospitable site where the infinitesimal fledgling plants can spring to life, because the conditions remain demanding. Monsoon storms must reach a crescendo. Although the seeds can absorb a certain amount of soil moisture, thus reducing by as much as a day the need for rain, germination between mid-July and mid-August requires at least two abundant rainstorms within two to five days.

South-facing slopes provide the most promising sites for the next step, germination. Coarse, gravely, airy soil is best; water-soaked dirt will not do. Hence, an unusually rainy summer does not necessarily translate into greater productivity. When, at last, optimal moisture and temperature coincide, germination takes two to three days. Even

then, each emerging saguaro infant must have an umbrella — a rock or nurse tree — to shade it from most of the summer sunlight.

Despite all these difficulties, a few seeds manage to remain on the ground through the winter, though they almost never contribute to the viable seed stock of the next year. In short, then, a sufficient supply of seeds must be provided each year in order to guarantee a stable, healthy number of individuals.

Central and southern Arizona, the plant's northernmost range, provide the potential for reproduction most years. There, the majority of summers seem to offer suitable conditions for germination. Other factors, after germination, limit the population. At no other time in the life of the saguaro are so many forfeited as during the one to five weeks between seedfall and the breaking open of the seed coats. But the hazards have just begun. A seedling looks nothing like the behemoth it could become. A succulent, spineless green blob of tulip-shaped tissue, the crown prince of the desert essentially eludes the naked eye.

Predators manage to sight it all the same. The farther away a seedling sprouts from the teeming faunal traffic around an adult plant, the better its chances for success. Wherever it arises, however, the thinly rooted new saguaro almost surely will be discovered and, if not eaten, at least uprooted. During these dry days, the vulnerable shoots become for predators more a source of water than of food. Insect larvae, newly hatched, bore into the base or the growing tip, leaving the skin a withering hulk. Packrats and desert mice attack it, too. Even if a fledgling cactus escapes these and withstands the rigors of the rainless early autumn, it is likely to succumb to hungry curved-billed thrashers, gilded flickers, or Gila woodpeckers. Many of these creatures shun cactuses if enough other greenery appears, an uncommon occurrence in the desert summer.

One experiment aptly illustrated the fate of even surviving seedlings. After a year, those grown in a commercial nursery stood about an inch tall and those in a lath house a little more than half that. Outdoors, the newcomers attained only slightly more than a tenth of an inch. But almost none reach that size. An average life expectancy for a new saguaro in the wild: less than six weeks. Fewer than one percent live longer.

And the rigorous challenges of early adulthood still lie ahead. ⬇

(TOP LEFT) *A paloverde nurse tree spreads protective arms over a youthful saguaro. If the saguaro survives the hazards of early life, it will outgrow and oftentimes inadvertently kill its nurse plant as the saguaro's widespread, shallow root system absorbs much of the available rainfall before it can reach the roots of its nurse.* DAVID ELMS, JR.

(LOWER LEFT) *Cracks in the rock provide sheltered growing space for this small saguaro, bottom, and young hedgehog cactus.* WESLEY HOLDEN

(LOWER RIGHT) *Friendly neighbor: a male Gambel's quail attains a lofty lookout.* PAUL BERQUIST

Evolution cleverly tailored the saguaro to survive in a setting hostile to most life. But the strategies utilized by the Sonoran Desert's trademark to endure turn out to be complex. For example, how quickly the cactus soars to great stature actually depends as much on *when* rains strike as *the amount* that showers the desert.

In human terms, the pace of the saguaro's growth proves inexorably slow. In addition to moist soil, the growing cactus requires warmth. So most growth, which is decidedly seasonal, comes with the monsoons of July, August, and September, sometimes surging within hours after the first heavy summer storm. If a heavy rain follows a prolonged dry spell, the desiccated trunk can absorb water at a phenomenal rate. Not surprisingly, though, the effect is cumulative; total summer growth hinges on the frequency of such rains.

Aridity inhibits progress during the virtually rainless autumn and spring. While winter cold limits growth, especially along the northernmost fringe of the saguaro range, some stem-size increase may take place during December and January rains if temperatures rise enough.

In common with the other columnar cactuses, saguaros change in appearance as they develop. At about 2.2 inches in height, the plants look like miniature baseball bats. At around 78 inches they resemble bowling pins, a shape that lasts until branching begins at about age 65. Then the top starts to taper, the upper trunk becoming thinner until the adult cactus, graced with arms, can be likened to an enormous bouquet.

Ordinarily, as saguaros reach maturity, arms

(LEFT) *Rodent's-eye-view of a multi-armed individual in Finger Rock Canyon, Santa Catalina Mountains. Those at higher, more moist locations put out more branches than their relatives elsewhere. In an unusually dry spot, though, one may not branch at all.* PETER KRESAN

(ABOVE) *A promising saguaro grows out of the bursage nurse plant that sheltered it over the first perilous years.* WESLEY HOLDEN

emerge where the trunk is thickest. No one knows with certainty why they arise precisely where they do, but branching means more water storage as well as prolific fruiting, and consequently ensures ensuing generations. Natural selection smiles on those plant strains that produce seeds most profusely.

Saguaros at cooler, higher elevations present more branches than those at lower, warmer sites simply because more moisture is available to them. Three times as many arms can be counted at Saguaro National Park East, near Tucson, than at Organ Pipe Cactus National Monument to the southwest on the Mexican border.

Not much has been pinned down about the rate at which arms reach out. Measurements were made of arm lengths of 10 specimens at Saguaro National Park East. Those branches grew slightly more than two inches one year and nearly three inches the next. Why some branches writhe into exotic shapes is an unanswered question, but the reason some arms droop, is freezing. Steenbergh and Lowe point out that cold temporarily dries out and weakens the plant tissue. Usually the branch eventually recovers and its tip begins to grow upward again.

Woody flute-like ribs, which provide the saguaro's superstructure, appear after approximately seven years. Young saguaros have 10 to 13 of them, the number increasing with age until there are 20 to 30 in the stem and 15 or more in the arms.

The young saguaro's growth rate accelerates as it stretches skyward, at least until it first flowers at about age 30. After that it spends up to half its resources, which previously went into growth, on blossoming and fruiting. Steenbergh and Lowe arrived at this figure by stripping the buds off some experimental plants, then comparing the growth with plants left untouched.

Even within a single locality, growth varies because of genetics, topography, the makeup of soil, and variations in sunlight exposure between north- and south-facing slopes. Plants are twice as dense on the south side of Wasson Peak in the Tucson Mountains as on the north.

(LEFT) *An early spring storm swirls above Saguaro National Park West.* JEFF GNASS

(TOP) *Young saguaros are bat-shaped. They fare best on stony slopes and almost never occupy the deep, water-washed (alluvial) soil of valleys.* DAVID ELMS, JR.

(ABOVE) *"Bowling pin" configuration characterizes plants after they reach some 78 inches in height.* WESLEY HOLDEN

The greatest differences can be seen in separate swaths of the Sonoran Desert. Everywhere, saguaro life expectancy mounts as the plants mature. But since saguaros depend on moisture and warmth, those growing in the wetter eastern portion of their range and in the warmer south generally fare twice as well as those to the drier west, or the cooler higher elevations and extreme northern reaches of its range.

In the cooler reaches of the saguaro's range, freezes frequently stunt growth, particularly among plants four years old or younger. By damaging the crowns, a severe cold spell can slow advancement for several years, thereby diminishing somewhat the advantage of more moisture.

In the hottest and thirstiest region of the saguaro's range, the Gran Desierto southeast of Yuma, saguaros are even more scarce, existing mainly along the streams and washes.

Taking all this into consideration, the relationship of age and height offers some basis for calculations, but it cannot be applied from one locale to another. Although this long has been evident, Steenbergh and Lowe confirmed it with data on some 2,500 saguaros, taken over 34 years. Many of the samples they measured themselves, using precision calipers and, for larger specimens, an ingenious telescoping aluminum pole-caliper.

They established that on the western slopes of the Rincon Mountains, at Saguaro National Monument East, 10-year-old juvenile saguaros average nearly three inches high. But across the city at Saguaro National Monument West, which receives almost two inches less rain per year, most youngsters the same age reach barely an inch and a half high. And at still drier Organ Pipe Cactus National Monument on the Arizona-Mexico border, decade-old saguaros stand little more than an inch.

With age, such manifestations become even more marked. These are approximations, but at age 50, a future giant should thrust upward a bit above 12 feet at Saguaro East, a little more than half that at Saguaro West, and only a bit above three feet at Organ Pipe.

At the century mark the same rough proportions are evident: 30, 24, and 15 feet. As with so many of the intricacies enshrouding the cactus Goliaths, determining their age in relation to their size is not easy.

PRECIPITATION

Elevations and summer and annual
precipitation for saguaro habitat.

	SNPE	SNPW	OPCNM
Elevation	3,100'-4,500'	2,560'-4,600'	1,670'-4,800'
Summer rain	5.29"	4.44"	4.02"
Annual rain	12.30"	10.27"	7.56"

SNPE:	Saguaro National Park East
SNPW:	Saguaro National Park West
OPCNM:	Organ Pipe Cactus National Monument

(LEFT ABOVE) *Abundant paloverde trees typify the
luxuriant desert growth of the Tucson Mountains. Not far
from the relatively rainy northeastern boundary of the
saguaro's growing region, annual rainfall here averages
10.27 inches.*

(ABOVE) *By contrast, survival proves difficult on the
parched sands of western Arizona near Yuma. Here in only
four out of every 100 years is there enough rainfall for
seedlings to establish themselves. Average annual rainfall
in Yuma? 2.99 inches.* PHOTOGRAPHS BY PETER KRESAN

SAGUARO GROWTH

Average heights by age of saguaros.
In inches through age 20, then by feet.

Years	SNPE	SNPW	OPCNM
1	.14"	.09"	.10"
2	.20"	.13"	.14"
3	.29"	.18"	.19"
4	.41"	.26"	.26"
5	.58"	.36"	.34"
10	2.70"	1.54"	1.03"
15	8.20"	4.16"	2.34"
20	17.80"	8.49"	4.41"
25	2.64'	1.23'	0.60'
30	4.14'	1.93'	0.91'
35	5.93'	2.85'	1.30'
40	7.94'	3.98'	1.77'
45	10.07'	5.32'	2.31'
50	12.27'	6.86'	2.91'
75	22.52'	15.92'	8.13'
100	30.37'	24.07'	15.88'
125	36.81'	30.32'	22.81'
150	41.79'	35.13'	28.52'

Based on *Ecology of the Saguaro III,* by Steenbergh and Lowe.

TALL...TALLER... TALLEST?

Somewhere out on Arizona's sere landscape must rule the loftiest saguaro of all, one yet unmeasured. Meanwhile, until such an ultimate specimen turns up — if it does — claims continue for the grandest of all.

In the mid-1970s the greatest height for a scientifically measured standing saguaro giant was one slightly under 53 feet. It lorded over a south-facing slope in the Tucson Mountains. Two months after Paul Fugate photographed it at the end of June 1975, a storm severed the plant near its base, and the three-armed patriarch was dead.

A saguaro near Cave Creek, north of Phoenix, was said to stand 78 feet. *The Guinness Book of World Records* duly proclaimed it the tallest. But after a 1986 windstorm toppled it, a neighbor reported that he had measured the saguaro's height posthumously and it reached only 58 feet.

In the 1996 edition, the Guinness book called a 57-foot 11-inch saguaro southwest of Phoenix the "tallest cactus." But the last measurement before it fell showed it to be nearly 59 feet. With that giant gone, the search goes on for the new tallest saguaro towering over the other denizens of the Sonoran Desert. ✿

(BELOW) *A cristate arm distinguishes a 44-foot tall giant near Four Peaks.* DAVID ELMS, JR.

(RIGHT) *In a remote desert region south of Phoenix, this saguaro stands 48 feet 10 inches high.* WESLEY HOLDEN

(OPPOSITE) *In 1989* The Guinness Book of World Records *listed this example, at 57 feet, 11 inches, to be the loftiest of all. Measured again in January, 1991, it had grown to nearly 59 feet tall. This "tallest saguaro" has since fallen.* ROBERT FAIRFIELD AND DENNIS WELLS

The tall mothers stand there
The tall mothers stand there
Whitely they flower
Black the blossoms dry
Red they ripen.

— A Tohono O'odham (Papago)
saguaro-growing song.

Once a small Tohono O'odham boy offered to cast a stone to dislodge a ripe red fruit high atop a tall saguaro. But an old woman of the tribe admonished the lad, reminding him that saguaros "are Indians, too. You don't do anything to hurt them."

Untold generations before the earliest Spaniards rode north from Mexico, the colossal cactus had become a tree of life for the Indians of the Southwest, and particularly for the Tohono O'odham, the Desert People. The O'odham nudged the fruit from lofty branches with lashed-together segments of willowy saguaro ribs. They then converted the bounty into seed flour, jam, and syrup, among a dozen different edibles — foods to sustain them through the hadean summer until their bean, corn, and squash crops matured in autumn. (In more modern times, they also feed saguaro seeds to their chickens.)

Saguaro motifs often adorned baskets, woven from yucca, catclaw, and other desert flora. Woody ribs of the fallen plant became construction material used to build bird cages, rough furniture, yard fences, and roofs. The hardy, callus-formed "boots," or tree-holes, often found strewn among saguaro skeletons, became handy containers.

Yet its symbolism loomed far larger than the plant's utility among the people the Spaniards named Papago. In Anglo culture the constellation Ursa Major is known as the Big Dipper, but to the natives of the Sonoran Desert it was "The Cactus Puller."

(LEFT) *An early summer sunset silhouettes fruit and withering blossoms atop the saguaros.* JACK DYKINGA

(ABOVE) *The prehistoric Hohokam etched seashells with acid extracted from the saguaro fruit.* JERRY JACKA

Some believed the first saguaro sprang from beads of sweat that dropped into the dust from the brow of I'itoi, the Elder Brother of the tribal pantheon. In another version, a boy neglected by his mother sank into a tarantula hole and emerged as a saguaro. Either way, placentas, to invoke longevity among newborns, may have been buried beneath the "sacred trees." And in the ultimate tribute, saguaro ribs sometimes lined graves.

Time was when, with each spring equinox, special songs were sung in a night-long ceremony to guarantee a proliferation of saguaro fruit. To the O'odham, the plant is "mashad." June, or "hahshanie mashad," the month of ripening fruit, began their traditional year. And the apex of that cycle came each August with the ritualistic drinking of saguaro-fruit wine.

In olden times, gathering the fruit was a family expedition, usually focused on cactus camps passed from generation to generation. Families trudged great distances, burdened with large clay pots — ollas — as well as baskets, beans, dried rabbit meat, water, other necessities.

A virtual race for the fruit took place between human harvesters and birds. But the O'odham believed the birds deserved a share. To frighten them away would bode ill. Felling the fruit and sorting and boiling it took one to three weeks. That was women's work, while the men hunted rabbits and supplied mesquite and ironwood for the fire. Special straining baskets, formed from leaves of desert spoon or sotol, separated juice from seeds and pulp. Once the pulp was scraped free, the husk was left on the ground inside out — pulp side up — an act thought to encourage rain.

All this came at a season when little else, save for mesquite beans and wild game, remained to sustain the people. By one estimate 600 families would have gathered up to 450,000 pounds of saguaro fruit a year; 20 to 30 pounds of fruit were needed to produce a gallon of reddish-brown, molasses-like syrup. Fermenting syrup into wine, which the men did, usually required four days. Some scholars say that except for a relatively low alcohol content — slightly less than 5 percent — saguaro wine can be likened in taste to that made by commercial vintners. To others it affronts the palate.

Like the rain-making ceremony to which it led, wine making was a communal effort, each family contributing syrup. The ritual itself was an important social event, and a moment for thanksgiving. I'itoi, it was related, instructed the Desert People to drink the wine "just as the earth drinks rain." Custom dictated every step. Memorized oratory, passed on from generation to generation, described the saguaro's life and how the plant saved the tribe from starvation before the Tohono O'odham learned to farm. One speech detailed the saguaro's influence on the "rain house," which harbored the wind, rain, and seeds.

Elders facing the cardinal directions, point by point, prayed for rain. Participants sat in specific spots. Lore even prescribed the way the wine was distributed. A person was offered a drink. One did not ask.

Inevitably, of course, time transforms all societies. Once, the Indians walked from their summer villages to areas where the cactus appeared most fruitful. Then the Spaniards introduced horses and wagons. Today they climb into their pickups and drive to a place where they can collect all the fruit they want in a day. Native plants are now treats, not necessities.

Nonetheless, wine ceremonies, if fewer in number, still continue. After all, the beneficence of *Carnegiea gigantea* can be traced back into the mists of antiquity. Before the O'odham, the Hohokam reigned over central and southern Arizona for almost 12 centuries after the birth of Christ.

The Hohokam utilized saguaros in many of the same ways as the O'odham. There is, however, a striking exception. Seashells, bartered from tribes along the Pacific Coast and Gulf of California, have been unearthed at many Hohokam ruins. Incised on some shells were the forms of animals and other designs. Because analyses proved the shells were not cut with tools, archaeologist Emil Haury pondered a possibility: Could the pictures have been engraved with acetic acid — vinegar — the product of wine left to sour?

He experimented. He allowed saguaro wine to turn to acid. After carving figures into the paraffin with which he coated shells, he treated them with the acid. Eureka! His specimens were indistinguishable from the artifacts.

Later, Haury and his colleagues excavated Snaketown, a sprawling Hohokam settlement beside the Gila River, southeast of Phoenix. There they found his *piece de resistance*, a prehistoric shell carved and painted with pitch but, for some reason, never bathed in the chemical. Abetted by the saguaro, the Hohokam had learned to etch with acid centuries before European artisans perfected the process.

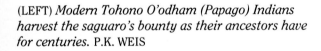

(LEFT) *Modern Tohono O'odham (Papago) Indians harvest the saguaro's bounty as their ancestors have for centuries.* P.K. WEIS

(TOP) *Tohono O'odham artist Michael Chiago depicts a saguaro fruit harvest. For centuries,* Carnegiea gigantea *has bestowed on the first Arizonans a veritable cornucopia: fruit and seed for food and drink, ribs for building materials, and "boots" for storage vessels.*

(ABOVE LEFT) *Long poles made from light but strong saguaro ribs are used to dislodge ripe red fruit.* P.K. WEIS

(ABOVE RIGHT) *Unlike most cactus fruit, that of the saguaro splits open easily when ripe.* DAVID ELMS, JR.

(RIGHT) *Finally, the sweet pulp is cooked and made into jam and wine.* P.K. WEIS

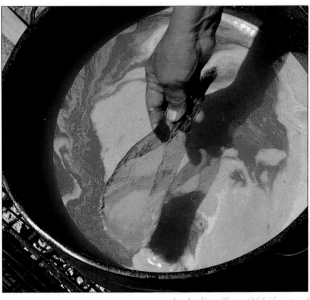

Saguaros were incidental victims of Tucson's frontier soldiers and settlers. In their most elaborate fantasies, neither the military nor the pioneer civilians could have foreseen such a toll. And while no one intentionally bothered the plant itself, the effect, though indirect, appears profound.

The government strung military installations across the Arizona Territory to subdue hostile Indians. One of the busiest was Fort (later Camp) Lowell at Tucson, established in 1862 by the California Volunteers in pursuit of Confederates. Lowell lasted until 1891, five years after Geronimo surrendered in Skeleton Canyon, on the Mexican border.

Among the pervasive military and civilian needs over all those years were firewood for fuel and lime for construction, items most readily available in the foothills of the Rincon and Santa Catalina mountains, east of the village. Pioneer Tucsonans quickly became aware of what the Mexicans had learned long before, that mesquite trees make the best firewood. Old mesquite stumps still dot the brows of the Santa Catalinas and Rincons, testimony to the appetite of early-era woodcutters.

On the other hand, the fuel of choice to fire the kilns to wrest lime from limestone was slow-burning paloverde. Because paloverde decays rapidly and leaves no stumps, one can merely imagine how many were felled in the Rincons for this purpose. The number must have been great.

The Rincon Mountains happened to be the natural stage for today's Saguaro National Park,

selected by the National Park Service because it bristled with the thickest saguaro forest known. Unfortunately the mesquite and paloverde the woodcutters removed from this very area were the prime shade source, also called "nurse trees," beneath which future cactuses should have sprung to life.

More than a century after the Army closed Fort Lowell and the woodcutters ceased their unwitting destruction, scholars attempting to fathom the biography of the saguaro cannot estimate the extent of the depredation. Because of the paucity of cactuses that germinated during pioneer days, though, their educated hunch is that it was significant.

After many millenia over which only natural forces endangered them, the saguaros now had felt man's hand. But another menace waited in the wings. The cattle were coming.

With the end of the Civil War, Texas stockmen began driving vast herds into Arizona in search of new pastures. By the 1890's, tens of thousands of the animals swarmed the Tucson area alone, a plague of insatiable grazing machines.

There were far more cattle than the fragile landscape could sustain, and their legacy has been thoroughly documented. Grasslands were denuded, often forever. Then storms scoured away the naked topsoil and incised gullies where none had existed. In places, networks of new arroyos branched and rebranched across entire regions, to become yawning, parched scars most of each year.

What this meant to the saguaro's fate is difficult to discern, in part because the consequences of overgrazing are difficult to distinguish from those of climatic change. Nonetheless, scientists contend the cattle decreased the density of many saguaro stands by trampling small plants, ravaging multitudes of mesquites and paloverdes, and, most critically, upsetting the desert's delicate ecological balance. That would be particularly tragic in flat country with few rocks to shade the seedlings.

Although the land often heals when livestock are excluded from savaged terrain, as at the parks, recovery can require generations. And other plants

(LEFT) *A moody winter storm and Praying Hands formation in the Superstition Mountains symbolize a natural requiem for a fallen giant.*
CHRISTINE KEITH

(ABOVE) *Gnarled yet stout, ribs provide a greater surface area than smooth skin, thus enhancing plant productivity. Saguaro ribs begin developing at about age seven, and those on the north side of the cactus are wider and shallower than those on south and southeast sides. No one knows why.* GILL KENNY

that appear may not be conducive to saguaro reproduction. At the least, overgrazing, like woodcutting, left a gap in cactus continuity.

Nor were humans through. Despite law-enforcement efforts, illegal trade in cactuses lingers. But the problem of poaching ran especially rampant early in this century, only a few years after the flood of livestock ebbed. The area that later would become Saguaro National Park East was a favored hunting ground.

Nearby residents reported a virtual mob of cactus pirates, inspired by a lush market among collectors and people who wanted the plants for landscaping. The most transportable and marketable size for the poachers would have been specimens 10 to 30 years old. That is a size, after the hazards of adolescence and before the rigors of old age, at which a saguaro is most likely to endure. And it was a size noticeably absent when the Monument was established. While losses can never be accurately computed, Warren Steenbergh and Charles Lowe cite evidence they were considerable.

If thievery has subsided, vandalism has not.

Among our less couth citizens are those who tend to shoot arrows or bullets into saguaros and cut, carve, or otherwise deface them.

In the early 1980's, a hunter on an outing near Lake Pleasant, north of Phoenix, fired his shotgun point blank at one. The giant collapsed onto the man, killing him instantly. From conversations overheard in the days that followed, one could gather many people were on the saguaro's side.

Although villainy probably lurks in no more souls than it ever did — per capita — the chances of mischief have increased simply because there are many more people. Arizona's population has burgeoned enormously since World War II. Statutes dictate that saguaros in the path of progress must be replanted elsewhere. That spares most of the present population. But hundreds of thousands of acres that might have given succor to saguaros yet unborn have been bulldozed, concreted, and paved.

For future generations of the long-lived saguaro, these latest incursions may mean much, little, or nothing. It is a question that will not be answered in our own lifetime.

(OPPOSITE) *A saguaro's ribs not only support the plant's mass, but also help distribute nutrients. Sometimes, even after death, the sturdy skeleton remains standing for years.* DAVID MUENCH

(ABOVE, LEFT) *During times of drought, rodents, usually thirsty rabbits, gnaw away at the base of young saguaros to get at the moist pulp. Such "girdling" doesn't destroy plants immediately but makes them more susceptible to freezing and wind damage. Wood rats, the only mammals that can survive almost solely on saguaro tissue, sometimes tunnel up the trunk. Ultimately, this young plant is mortally wounded.*

(ABOVE RIGHT) *One cannot help but be amazed at the saguaro's will to live. This photo shows new growth on the stump of a seemingly lifeless giant.*

(RIGHT) *Death notice: slime pools beneath a doomed adult. While saguaros suffer from few diseases, freezes, windstorms, and bacterial decay can kill them.* PHOTOGRAPHS BY DAVID ELMS, JR.

CATCHING CACTUS RUSTLERS

No smart thief would have stolen that saguaro. It stood 14 feet tall, weighed two tons and, more to the point, was an uncommon cristated specimen so distinctive people drove miles to photograph it. Neighbors named it Old Granddad. In January 1986, a wintering couple from Oregon reported that Old Granddad no longer lived near Quartzsite where he had resided 150 years or longer.

Yuma agents of the U.S. Fish and Wildlife Service, called into the case by Arizona authorities, were able within two months to trace the pilfered plant to a Las Vegas nursery, recover it, and arrest the Salome, Arizona, couple who had pirated it. The man served two years in prison and his wife got five years probation. The cristate saguaro was transplanted to the Desert Botanical Garden in Phoenix, where, weakened by its ordeal, it died a year and a half later. The Oregon residents received a $2,000 reward.

The case illustrates handsomely the wages of sin. The robbers sold their booty for $1,300 to a middleman, who somehow affixed an Arizona tag assuring its legality. In turn, the middleman (released for lack of evidence) wholesaled the cactus to the Nevada nursery for $1,500. The retail price there was $15,000.

Collectors prize cactuses, saguaros especially, and most of all the crowned freaks. Because it pays so well, cactus rustling runs rampant. Quite literally, there is a crime wave against Nature. Sting operations by federal and state sleuths in 1990 trapped 23 other Arizona saguaro stealers. Most of those defendants, like the Salome man, were convicted under a national law, the 1900 Lacey Act, that punishes people who move across state lines any plant or animal taken in violation of state statutes.

Arizona's law, enacted in 1927 and repeatedly updated, is one of the toughest anywhere, affording guardianship — in different degrees — for all wild plants. But saguaros, senitas, and organ pipes are among more than two dozen "highly safeguarded" cactus species. In the language of the law, "their prospects, in the foreseeable future, for survival... are in danger of extinction."

Without an Arizona Department of Agriculture permit, they cannot be collected or mutilated on public land or even be moved for sale from private property. Violators can be fined up to $10,000.

Several Arizona museums and botanical gardens sell saguaro seed to patient hobbyists, along with small nursery-grown plants, and homeowners can purchase large ones from nurseries. Such plants usually are salvaged legally from construction sites. They still must be sold with state tags, and buyers certainly should not try to transplant them outside the monarch's native region. Some advice from experts: Start fairly small.

In 1990, inspectors from the Arizona Commission for Agriculture and Horticulture, which was replaced at the beginning of 1991 by the State Department of Agriculture, confiscated 524 plants, about a tenth of them saguaros. The commission cannot say whether more cactus rustlers are at work these days, but more of them are being caught.

The U.S. attorney for Arizona who prosecuted the felons snared in the 1990 sting, said the office "remains ever mindful of our role in the stewardship of Arizona's unique and fragile flora and fauna." ◢

(ABOVE) *These plants were salvaged from a road improvement project and made available for purchase at Desert Botanical Garden in Phoenix. Saguaros are a protected species and law requires state-issued permit tags to move them. Fully mature plants with arms require large equipment as the cactuses are incredibly heavy. When scientists weighed a fallen giant northeast of Tucson, it tipped the scales at nine tons.*

(RIGHT) *Commercially grown saguaros are potted and sold at Desert Botanical Garden, Phoenix; Boyce Thompson Arboretum, Superior; Arizona-Sonora Desert Museum, Tucson; and at some nurseries.*
PHOTOGRAPHS BY DAVID ELMS, JR.

Circular holes often appear high up a saguaro's trunk. These actually are nesting holes carved into the stem, and Gila woodpeckers and their cousins, gilded flickers, are their architects and builders.

Biologist Oscar H. Soule made these observations: "The actual construction is carried out by both males and females. The bird holds itself on the lip of the hole...leans into the hole and drums the saguaro flesh with its beak. It either grasps a loose piece of tissue with its beak or the piece sticks to the beak due to the plant fluids; the bird then brings it to the mouth of the hole. If the chunk is large...it will be flicked over the shoulder."

Once their eggs hatch inside and their brood is raised, the excavators never use the cavity again. But they have unveiled the saguaro to a multitude of links on the food chain, from the microscopic to the obvious. (Cactus wrens, the state bird, nest in the elbows where arms poke out from the trunk. So do white-winged doves, red-tailed hawks and others.)

After the original tenants abandon the hole, a succession of other birds follows. Day-sleeping elf owls, the smallest of their species in the United States, move into some openings. Ash-throated and Arizona flycatchers nest in others, as do Lucy's warblers, purple martins, and an occasional cactus wren.

Many ornithologists believe hole nesting indicates an evolutionary advancement for birds. If this is true, the woodpeckers and flickers may have helped the other species to evolve. While woodpecker and flicker eggs generally rest on the bare floor of the excavation, maximizing its natural shelter, two species, house finches and starlings, carry in twigs and grass to make nests. This foreign matter only diminishes the primary advantages the

(LEFT) *Home on the range: a cactus wren family nests inside a saguaro treehole.* C. ALLAN MORGAN

(ABOVE) *An elf owl, the world's smallest owl, makes its home in one of the world's largest cactuses.* PAUL A. BERQUIST

holes offer — concealment.

Very little was known of these advantages, and even less about the recondite micro-world of saguaro treeholes, until Soule and Richard D. Krizman studied them in the early 1960's. Among the information their research provided was that temperatures within the chambers are milder and vary less dramatically than those of the outside air.

Because saguaros are 90 percent water, these chambers are virtually encapsulated in insulating envelopes of watery tissue. When the temperature of the surrounding air reaches its height, the holes remain comparatively cool. As the ambient air cools after dusk, the saguaro body holds some heat. And at a time when shade on the desert is most precious, at midday during the summer, almost no solar rays reach the lowest depths of the hole.

The birds are not alone. Bats and even a gopher snake have turned up in treeholes.

Such refuges naturally attract an array of insects. During warm months, the holes literally hum. Katydids and desert grasshoppers drop in to elude the searing heat. Plant-eating beetles co-exist with other beetles that consume animal remnants. Since the holes often hold water after showers, mosquitoes proliferate. Spiders spin webs. Gnats, bedbugs, moths, and wasps abound. So do pseudoscorpions, probably brought in on the legs of the flies that feed on them. However, the most common insect found in these cavities is the wingless, primitive springtail, so named because of wire-like abdominal appendages that allow it to leap long distances.

Soule and Krizman thought that the holes seldom damage the plant. When birds begin pecking away, an innate chemical defense is unleashed, enabling the saguaro to defend itself. UofA chemist Roger Lee Caldwell identified one of the strategic defenders, conceivably the front-line force, as the adrenalin-like compound called dopamine.

When the cactus is attacked, a metabolic alarm rapidly steps up the production of this compound, normally in the cortex, the major fleshy part of the plant outside the inner circlet of wooden ribs. Dopamine rushes outward to surround the site of the stress, and there causes the buildup of a thick cork-like callus that serves to seal off the cactus from further harm. The principle is not dissimilar to that of scar tissue.

Upon exposure to air, dopamine darkens. Melanin, the same substance that puts the dark pigment in human skin, also forms around the wound, and the armor of cork turns almost jet in hue. Often the size of a football, the astonishingly durable callus boots, the legacy of woodpeckers and flickers, linger intact on the ground years after the saguaro itself succumbs to age, and even the ribs have returned to dust.

Early in the 1980's, two decades after Soule and Krizman, two other scientists used the callus boots to assess the architecture of the hatcheries the birds sculpt inside saguaros.

It turned out that the holes look quite different, depending upon which species constructs them. Being smaller, the red-pated Gila woodpecker needs less space, and its sturdy, chisel-tipped beak perfectly suits the task. Woodpeckers build their nests in the plump lower part of the plant, entirely within the soft outer tissue.

But the ground-feeding gilded flicker, recognizable by its cinnamon cap, has a slim, pointed bill fine for snaring ants and other insects but poorly designed for chiseling. So flickers must dig high up on the saguaro stem, where the woody skeleton is thinner. Their larger nests push through the skeleton, often even going out the other side.

Such damage, Joseph R. McAuliffe and Paul Hendricks concluded, "often directly and indirectly" sounds a death knell for a cactus giant.

(BELOW) *Legacy of a treehole: the callus-hard boot of a gilded flicker lies amid a crumbling saguaro skeleton. Note the holes where the boot touched the severed ribs.* DAVID ELMS, JR.

(RIGHT ABOVE) *Different excavators carve out different size treeholes. The gilded flicker makes large holes in the upper portion of the saguaro's trunk or arms, actually severing the ribs.* PAUL A. BERQUIST

(RIGHT BELOW) *The Gila woodpecker's nest is smaller and usually lower on the trunk. The boot is up against the ribs, not cut into them.* C. ALLAN MORGAN

ILLUSTRATIONS BY WENDY HODGESON

What happened? Meg Weesner, chief of science and resource management at the park says the thick stands of saguaros for which the park is famous resulted from late 1800s when conditions were perfect. But the harvesting of fuel wood and cattle grazing drastically altered the habitat, preventing a generation of saguaros from reproducing.

With the establishment of the Monument in the 1930s, land use changed. Cattle were removed in the late 1950s, and by the 1970s, the first young saguaros began appearing, and they have thrived ever since. Weesner says the ability of those young plants to survive is directly related to under-story vegetation — shrubs, grasses and trees that protect them from frost, heat, and predation.

Since 1990, the per-acre population of saguaros at the park is again on the rise. But the news isn't all good. "Continuing development outside the park is taking out more and more saguaro habitat and making it into yards, shopping centers, and roads," says Weesner. "Once land is developed, it no longer has the whole complement of vegetation needed for small saguaros to become established."

At other areas around Tucson — such as Tumamoc Hill, where scientists have been monitoring saguaros for nearly a century — young ones aren't growing fast enough to maintain the current stand, and experts aren't sure why.

Other problems persist. Thirsty rodents gnaw at the bases of the plant and there has been a decimation among the bats that participate in pollination. One scientist has suggested that depletion of the earth's ozone level has brought more exposure to ultraviolet radiation that harms plants.

But no one is ringing bells of alarm. After all, the study that Alcorn, Orum, and others are continuing began with the United State Department of Agriculture in 1940, and questions still remain.

"We've had 55 annual surveys, but we still need to keep doing them," says Orum. "It's important to get a long look because the next 50 years will probably put us in entirely new territory."

In other words, this monarch of desert species could very well outlive our own.

(ABOVE) *Desertscape: Prickly pears and saguaros share a verdant swath of cactus country.*
KATHLEEN NORRIS COOK

ACKNOWLEDGEMENTS

Carle Hodge drew heavily upon — and was enormously indebted to — the three-volume *Ecology of the Saguaro,* by Warren F. Steenbergh and Charles H. Lowe. These are 1976, 1977, and 1983 publications of the National Park Service.

Indian uses of saguaros are summarized by Frank S. Crosswhite, director of the Boyce Thompson Southwestern Arboretum near Superior, Arizona, in the Spring 1980 issue of the arboretum quarterly, *Desert Plants.* Also in that issue is an excellent bibliography on saguaro ethnobotany by Bernard L. Fontana.

Papago Indian Religion, a 1946 book by ethnologist Ruth M. Underhill, provided the Tohono O'Odham saguaro-growing song, and the story of the boy who wanted to hurl a rock at a saguaro fruit came from Gary Paul Nabhan.

Phyllis Morgan's bibliography (see inside back cover) led to some unfamiliar sources.

We also relied on the scientific reports of (and in some cases interviews with) Stanley M. Alcorn, Roger L.Caldwell, Arthur B. Gibson, James Rodney Hastings, Paul Hendricks, Karl E. Horak, Richard D. Krizman, George Olin, Joseph R. McAuliff, Oscar M. Soule, Cornelius Steelink, Raymond M. Turner, and Thomas R. Van Devender. Those sources are listed alphabetically.

Alcorn, Fontana, Olin, Turner, and Van Devender reviewed all or parts of the manuscript, as did George N. Knecht. Also, the writer is indebted to the editorial acumen of Sylvia Cody. The author accepts responsibility for any misinterpretations, however.

Finally, special thanks to Suzi Holden whose inquisitiveness inspired this book.

(ABOVE) *Stages of blossoming: buds, flowers, and withering blooms.* DAVID ELMS, JR.

(BACK COVER) *Summer storms building behind the Superstition Mountains east of Phoenix often sweep onto the desert below, bringing welcome rain to saguaros and other cactuses.* RICHARD STRANGE